★ It's My State! ★ ★ ★ ★ ★

INDIANA
The Hoosier State

Kathleen Kerzipilski, Richard Hantula, and Ruth Bjorklund

Cavendish
Square

New York

Published in 2017 by Cavendish Square Publishing, LLC
243 5th Avenue, Suite 136, New York, NY 10016

Library of Congress Cataloging-in-Publication Data

Names: Kerzipilski, Kathleen, author. | Hantula, Richard, author. | Bjorklund, Ruth, author.
Title: Indiana / Kathleen Kerzipilski, Richard Hantula, and Ruth Bjorklund.
Description: New York : Cavendish Square Publishing, 2016. | Series: It's my state! | Includes index. | Description based on print version record and CIP data provided by publisher; resource not viewed.
Identifiers: LCCN 2015049640 (print) | LCCN 2015049119 (ebook) | ISBN 9781627124997 (ebook) | ISBN 9781627124966 (library bound)
Classification: LCC F526.3 (print) | LCC F526.3 .K47 2016 (ebook) | DDC 977.2--dc23
LC record available at http://lccn.loc.gov/2015049640

Editorial Director: David McNamara
Editor: Fletcher Doyle
Copyeditor: Nathan Heidelberger
Art Director: Jeffrey Talbot
Designer: Alan Sliwinski
Production Assistant: Karol Szymczuk
Photo Research: J8 Media

INDIANA
CONTENTS

A Quick Look at Indiana 4

1. The Hoosier State 7
Indiana County Map 10
Indiana Population by County 11
10 Key Sites 14
10 Key Plants and Animals 20

2. From the Beginning 23
The Native People 26
Making a Woven Basket 30
10 Key Cities 34
10 Key Dates in State History 43

3. The People 45
10 Key People 48
10 Key Events 54

4. How the Government Works 57
Political Figures from Indiana 62
You Can Make a Difference 63

5. Making a Living 65
10 Key Industries 68
Recipe for Hoosier Corn Casserole 70

Indiana State Map 74
Indiana Map Skills 75
State Flag, Seal, and Song 76
Glossary 77
More About Indiana 78
Index 79

A QUICK LOOK AT

State Tree: Tulip Tree

The tulip tree is among the tallest trees in Indiana's forests. It can reach 164 feet (50 meters). This tree has clusters of bell-shaped flowers. The distinctive leaves of the tulip tree appear on the Indiana state seal. The tulip tree is also called the yellow poplar.

State Flower: Peony

The peony was chosen as the state flower in 1957. In the spring, the plants produce large, fragrant flowers in shades of white, pink, and red. Because of their beautiful flowers and dark green, glossy leaves, peonies are grown in gardens and yards throughout Indiana.

State Bird: Cardinal

The cardinal can be found in Indiana throughout the year. The male cardinal is easily identified by its bright red feathers and crest (the feathers that form a point at the top of its head). The female has brown feathers and a light red head and crest. Cardinals flit through shrubs, thickets, and trees. They eat a variety of insects, seeds, and small fruits.

INDIANA
POPULATION: 6,483,802

⭐ State Stone: **Salem Limestone**

Indiana limestone originated more than three hundred million years ago when the Midwest was under an inland sea. The limestone was formed from layers of microscopic **fossils** of the sea creatures. The beautiful, fine-textured stone is taken from quarries in central and southern Indiana. It has been used in buildings throughout the country

⭐ State River: **Wabash River**

The Wabash River and its valley have long attracted settlers and explorers. Many Native American towns and camps were located along the Wabash. The river's name comes from the Native Miami word *wah-ba-shi-ki*, which means "pure white." This probably referred to the limestone over which the river flows in its upper sections.

⭐ State Language: **English**

Indiana adopted English as the official language of the state in 1984. In Indiana—as in all the other states—government meetings are conducted in English, and official records and legal documents are written in English. In 1995, Indiana also gave official recognition to American Sign Language, the chief sign language used by deaf Americans.

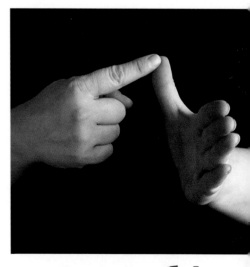

The top of Mount Baldy provides a beautiful view of Lake Michigan.

The Hoosier State

Indiana is located in the north-central part of the United States. Roughly rectangular in shape, Indiana is bounded on the north by Michigan and in the northwest corner by Lake Michigan, one of the Great Lakes. To the east lies the state of Ohio, and to the south are the Ohio River and the state of Kentucky. Indiana shares a western border with Illinois. Indiana has a total area of 36,420 square miles (94,326 square kilometers), of which 593 square miles (1,536 sq km) are water. In size, it is the thirty-eighth largest state. It is divided into ninety-two counties.

Shaped by Glaciers and a Sea

More than three hundred million years ago, much of North America was underwater. Over the past one million years, the northern part of the continent has experienced several periods when **glaciers**—large, slow-moving ice masses—formed and traveled over the land. As the glaciers moved, they shaped the land. Then, as the climate warmed, these masses of ice melted and retreated northward. Scientists think that the land that now includes Indiana has been under glaciers a number of times in the past one million years. Evidence of the ancient sea and the glaciers is visible in the geography of Indiana.

Water and great soil make for fertile farmland in Indiana.

Indiana Borders

North:	Michigan
	Lake Michigan
South:	Kentucky
East:	Ohio
	Kentucky
West:	Illinois

The movement of the glaciers left most of Indiana flat or rolling and covered with sandy, fertile soil called till. The pockets of marshes and ponds in the northern part of the state are another sign of the thawing glaciers. The glaciers carved up the land and left water behind. The sand dunes along the shores of Lake Michigan are made up of windblown debris that was created by past glaciers. As each glacier formed and then melted, it reshaped the region's rivers and the shoreline of Lake Michigan.

Southern Indiana was largely untouched by the glaciers, but it was affected by the great inland sea. While the land was underwater, layers of limestone and dolomite—a type of mineral—were laid down. These stones were easily dissolved and eroded by underground streams. The result is the hilly surface and the knobs, ravines, bluffs, and sinkholes found in southern Indiana. Streams disappear into the ground or emerge as springs. Many caves can be found underground. This type of landscape is called **karst**.

Dune Diversity

The sand dunes in the Indiana Dunes National Lakeshore on Lake Michigan rise to a height of nearly 200 feet (60 m). Mount Baldy, at 126 feet (38 m) high, is moving inward at an average rate of 4 feet (1.2 m) per year. It is the largest moving dune in the park. The national lakeshore, which covers about 15,000 acres (6,070 hectares), contains not only dunes but also oak grassland, swamps, marshes, prairies, rivers, forests, and beaches. In terms of number of species per acre, it features one of the most diverse collections of plants of any site managed by the US National Park Service. These species range from grasses to tall white pines to algae. More than 1,100 types of flowering plants and ferns live there.

Forests and Prairies

Most of Indiana's trees are **deciduous** hardwoods such as maple, elm, ash, beech, hickory, oak, cherry, walnut, and yellow poplar (also called tulip trees). In the autumn, the leaves of deciduous trees change color and fall from the branches. Trees that require the same kind of soil and moisture grow side by side in the same forest. Softwood trees such as cypress and cottonwood grow in some of the state's wetlands, most notably in the southwest.

Some two hundred years ago, forests covered more than 85 percent of what is now Indiana. However, by 1922, the forests were so extensively cut that the state forester predicted that Indiana would one day have no forests at all. That prediction proved to

The deciduous trees of Indiana are bare against the winter sky.

INDIANA
COUNTY MAP

INDIANA
POPULATION BY COUNTY

County	Population	County	Population	County	Population
Adams	34,387	Hendricks	145,448	Pike	12,845
Allen	355,329	Henry	49,462	Porter	164,343
Bartholomew	76,794	Howard	82,752	Posey	25,910
Benton	8,854	Huntington	37,124	Pulaski	13,402
Blackford	12,766	Jackson	42,376	Putnam	37,963
Boone	56,640	Jasper	33,478	Randolph	26,171
Brown	15,242	Jay	21,253	Ripley	28,818
Carroll	20,155	Jefferson	32,428	Rush	17,392
Cass	38,966	Jennings	28,525	St. Joseph	266,931
Clark	110,232	Johnson	139,654	Scott	24,181
Clay	26,890	Knox	38,440	Shelby	44,436
Clinton	33,224	Kosciusko	77,358	Spencer	20,952
Crawford	10,713	LaGrange	37,128	Starke	23,363
Daviess	31,648	Lake	496,005	Steuben	34,185
Dearborn	50,047	LaPorte	111,467	Sullivan	21,475
Decatur	25,740	Lawrence	46,134	Switzerland	10,613
DeKalb	42,223	Madison	131,636	Tippecanoe	172,780
Delaware	117,671	Marion	903,393	Tipton	15,936
Dubois	41,889	Marshall	47,051	Union	7,516
Elkhart	197,559	Martin	10,334	Vanderburgh	179,703
Fayette	24,277	Miami	36,903	Vermillion	16,212
Floyd	74,578	Monroe	137,974	Vigo	107,848
Fountain	17,240	Montgomery	38,124	Wabash	32,888
Franklin	23,087	Morgan	68,894	Warren	8,508
Fulton	20,836	Newton	14,244	Warrick	59,689
Gibson	33,503	Noble	47,536	Washington	28,262
Grant	70,061	Ohio	6,128	Wayne	68,917
Greene	33,165	Orange	19,840	Wells	27,636
Hamilton	274,569	Owen	21,575	White	24,643
Hancock	70,002	Parke	17,339	Whitley	33,292
Harrison	39,364	Perry	19,338		

Source: US Bureau of the Census, 2010

Bad Guests

Not all plants or animals are desirable. Some species, known as **invasive species**, prey on native species and/or destroy native habitats. Among them in Indiana are the feral hog, mute swan, Asian carp, gypsy moth, emerald ash borer, and zebra mussel.

be wrong, thanks largely to government programs encouraging forest growth. Instead, over the past century, the number of acres with trees has increased. Today, about 20 percent of the state has forests. Most of the trees are in the southern half of the state. William Hoover, a professor in the Department of Forestry and Natural Resources at Purdue University, has described the regrowth of the forests as "a tribute to the resiliency of nature."

People enjoy the beauty and seasonal changes of Indiana's forests. For many mammals, birds, and insects, the trees are needed for their survival. The forests are their habitat. Trees also help to clean the air and to prevent soil erosion. If too much soil erodes, or wears away, the nutrients in the soil are lost, and plants and trees would not be able to grow roots and survive. Trees are also valued for furniture making and construction material.

The tallgrass prairie of the central United States and Canada extends into northwest Indiana. At one time, prairie covered about 15 percent of Indiana. The prairie has marshy areas as well as sparse stands of shrubs and oaks. Fire is necessary to the life cycle of the prairie. The fires keep the prairie open, with few or no trees, so grasses and wildflowers can have all the sunlight they need. Grasses and prairie plants survive the fires because they have deep, widespread roots. Even if the tops of the plants are burned, the roots are safe and able to send up new green growth after the fire has been put out.

Most of Indiana's prairie and wetlands have been lost to development of farms, roads, buildings, and other structures. The soils remain, however, and they are now the basis of some of Indiana's richest farmland.

High and Big

The highest natural point in Indiana is the top of Hoosier Hill in Wayne County. It is 1,257 feet (383 m) above sea level. The lowest point, at 320 feet (98 m) above sea level, is in Posey County, where the Wabash River flows into the Ohio River. The tallest building in the state is the Chase Tower in Indianapolis. With a height of 830 feet (253 m), it is the tallest building in the Midwest outside Chicago and Cleveland. Indiana's largest natural

Lake Monroe, the largest artificial lake in Indiana, is a mecca for boaters in summer.

lake is Wawasee, in the northern part of the state. It has an area of more than 3,000 acres (1,214 ha). The largest artificial lake is Monroe, south of Bloomington. Its area is about 10,750 acres (4,350 ha).

Rivers and Water

Indiana has two main **watersheds**. A watershed is a large area that is drained by rivers and other bodies of water. One of the state's watersheds occupies a narrow strip across northern Indiana. Here, the rivers flow toward the Great Lakes. Their waters eventually reach the Saint Lawrence River, which continues to the Atlantic Ocean. The rivers of the other watershed flow toward the Ohio River or the Illinois River and then on to the Mississippi River and into the Gulf of Mexico.

The Saint Marys and the Saint Joseph Rivers drain part of northeastern Indiana. They meet to form the Maumee River. The Maumee flows through Ohio and empties into Lake Erie. The city of Fort Wayne grew at this junction of the three rivers. Another Saint Joseph River rises in southern Michigan, flows through

Wild Water

The Wabash River flows free of dams for 411 miles (661 km), the longest free-running river east of the Mississippi River.

Angel Mounds

Indiana Dunes National Lakeshore

Jasper-Pulaski Wildlife Area

1. Angel Mounds

Along the Ohio River near Evansville is one of the best-preserved prehistoric villages in North America. Ancestors of the region's Native Americans erected eleven large earthen mounds on 103 acres (42 ha) to elevate important buildings.

2. Forks of the Wabash

Prehistoric **nomads** used this major portage between the Great Lakes and the Mississippi River in Huntington. Later it was the home of the Miami tribe. In the 1830s, white settlers built, and soon abandoned, a 468-mile (753-kilometer) -long canal.

3. Hoosier National Forest

Hoosier National Forest protects 200,000 acres (80,900 ha) of hickory, oak, walnut, and hemlock forests around Indianapolis. Hikers and horseback riders enjoy 200 miles (322 km) of trails. Visitors also enjoy birding, swimming, boating, fishing, and wildlife viewing

4. Indiana Dunes National Lakeshore

Indiana Dunes National Lakeshore covers 15 miles (24 km) of beach along Lake Michigan and 15,000 acres (6,070 ha) of prairies, forests, and wetlands. You can hike up the shifting sands of Mount Baldy for an expansive view of the lake.

5. Jasper-Pulaski Wildlife Area

The Jasper-Pulaski Wildlife Area preserves 8,142 acres (3,295 ha) of wetlands for birds and game. In winter, flocks of giant sandhill cranes stop over during their migration. Tens of thousands arrive at once and somehow avoid colliding during landing.

6. Loblolly Marsh Nature Preserve

Indiana was covered in swamps and marshes before settlers drained the wetlands for farmland. Loblolly preserves the natural history of Indiana's wetlands and is home to many rare native plants and animals, such as the snowy owl and northern leopard frog.

7. Muscatuck National Wildlife Refuge

The Muscatuck National Wildlife Refuge provides a habitat of forests, grasslands, and wetlands for migrating and nesting birds. More than 280 species of birds stop over each year. The refuge also protects once common river otters.

Muscatuck National Wildlife Refuge

8. Portland Arch Nature Preserve

The Portland Arch Nature Preserve is a national natural landmark. Two streams meet and flow through a lightly forested ravine and massive walls of sandstone. The water carved a natural bridge called the Portland Arch.

Portland Arch Nature Preserve

9. Potawatomi Wildlife Park

The 317-acre (128 ha) Potawatomi Wildlife Park lies along the Tippecanoe River. The park protects native plants and animals. Visitors may tour Benack's Village, a former Potawatomi encampment.

10. Turkey Run State Park

Besides stately forests of pine, hickory, and oak, Turkey Run State Park has trails through sandstone ravines. Visitors also tour Colonel Richard Lieber's cabin (right). He is the "father" of Indiana's state park system, and he worked with Theodore Roosevelt to preserve the nation's natural resources.

Turkey Run State Park

Clifty Creek drops 60 feet (18 m) over Big Clifty Falls before flowing into the Ohio River.

extreme northern Indiana and returns to Michigan before emptying into Lake Michigan.

The industrial area in the northwest corner of Indiana is named the Calumet region after the Grand Calumet and the Little Calumet Rivers. These two slow-moving rivers empty into Lake Michigan. The rise of land separating them from the region draining into the Mississippi is called the Valparaiso **moraine**. It is a ridge of rubble left by one of the glaciers.

The Kankakee River crosses northwest Indiana and joins the Illinois River, which is a tributary of the Mississippi. French trappers and traders from Canada learned how to travel great distances from the Native Americans living along Indiana's rivers. From Canada, the trappers sailed across the Great Lakes to Lake Michigan until they reached the mouth of the Saint Joseph River. They paddled the Saint Joseph to the **portage** at South Bend. A portage is a trail used by people to carry their boats between two bodies of water. The portage ended at the Kankakee River, which flows into the Illinois River and then into the Mississippi River. Once on the Mississippi, the traders could go north, west to the frontier, or south to New Orleans to trade their goods.

The Wabash River is the major river of Indiana. It rises in Ohio, flows west across Indiana, and then turns south. It forms the southern half of Indiana's western boundary and becomes increasingly twisty. The Wabash meets the Ohio River at the southwest corner of Indiana. Tributaries of the Wabash include Sugar Creek and the Whitewater, Tippecanoe, Eel, and White Rivers. In southern Indiana, sand dunes edge sections of the Wabash and White Rivers. Indiana's water supply is drawn from groundwater (underground water), rivers, reservoirs, and streams.

Fossil beds along the shore of the Ohio River in Falls of the Ohio State Park contain the remains of creatures that lived hundreds of millions of years ago.

The Seasons

Indiana has four distinct seasons. Winters are cold, with an average temperature near freezing, or 32 degrees Fahrenheit (0 degrees Celsius). Snowstorms and ice are common, with the north of the state receiving more snow than the south. In spring, the days become longer and warmer. Summers are hot and humid. Day after day, the daytime temperature can stay above 90°F (32°C). Many summer days reach an uncomfortable level of humidity in the air of 80 percent. In the fall, the days grow shorter and cooler.

Indiana receives about 40 inches (100 centimeters) of precipitation each year. Most of this is in the form of rain. Indiana receives snowfall in averages of 20 to 30 inches (50 to 76 cm) a year, depending on region. South Bend averages about 66 inches (168 cm) of snow a year, whereas Tell City averages a mere 4.4 inches (11 cm). It takes about 1 inch (2.54 cm) of rain to make 8 inches (20.3 cm) of wet snow. Precipitation is measured by

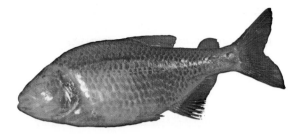

Eyeless cave fish have evolved to survive in underwater caverns with little or no light.

how much water is left when the snow melts. Thunderstorms can travel through Indiana, and tornadoes occasionally touch down, causing extensive damage to people, landscape, and buildings.

Wildlife

Some mammals found in Indiana include moles, shrews, chipmunks, squirrels, rabbits, bats, woodchucks, raccoons, and opossums. Beavers, once hunted for their fur, build their lodges in the state's ponds and streams. Foxes and bobcats are sometimes seen. Deer were plentiful in the early 1800s, but one hundred years later, they had almost disappeared from the state—a result of hunting and loss of habitat as more land was turned into farms or developed for other purposes. Authorities worked to rebuild and protect deer herds, and eventually deer became so numerous that the damage they caused to crops and trees became a problem. The number of motor vehicle accidents involving deer also increased. To keep the deer population in check, hunters using bows or guns are now allowed to harvest deer during certain times of the year.

Fish such as trout, bass, catfish, pike, and sunfish are plentiful in Indiana's lakes and streams. They provide food for wild animals, but they also make fishing popular in the state's bodies of water. Several state fish hatcheries have been in operation since the 1930s. They produce walleye, pike, bass, rainbow trout, and coho salmon for release into state waterways. Darters—a kind of small fish that lives in streams—and eyeless cave fish are rare and are not allowed to be fished for sport.

Many birds pass through Indiana on their annual migrations. Each year, millions of birds such as cranes, Canada geese, wood ducks, and warblers migrate from northern Canada southward thousands of miles to warmer regions for the winter. There are four paths, or **flyways,** in the United States and Canada. Indiana is part of the Mississippi Flyway. Each spring and fall, the birds stop at wetlands along the flyways to nest and feed. Many environmental groups are working together on **conservation** programs to protect more than 30,000 acres (12,140 ha) of Indiana's wetlands.

Many birds are year-round residents, such as nuthatches, cardinals, juncos, and purple finches. Wading birds and ducks, such as bitterns and mallards, frequent the marshes and ponds. Meadowlarks, orioles, wrens, sparrows, robins, blue jays, thrushes,

More lupine is being planted to increase the habitat of the Karner blue butterfly.

woodpeckers, and flickers are common on the edges of fields and in wooded areas. Birds of prey, such as owls, hawks, and peregrine falcons, hunt small animals and other birds. Osprey and bald eagles are rare, though wildlife experts are working to increase the population of these large birds.

Endangered Species in Indiana

Habitat loss is the main reason that plants and animals become rare or **extinct** (a type of plant or animal that is extinct has completely died out). In Indiana, the landscape has changed since the early pioneer days. As a result, certain species are extinct or **endangered** (at risk of becoming extinct). In other instances, some species survive only in certain areas.

Indiana has several endangered species, including the piping plover and the least tern, both of whose wetlands habitats have been polluted or overdeveloped. There are eleven species of mussels that are endangered due to the zebra mussel, an invasive species from Asia that arrived stuck to the hulls of cargo ships. Zebra mussels eat all the nutrients that baby fish and other mussels need to survive.

The Karner blue butterfly is one of the endangered species of Indiana. The wings of this small and pretty butterfly are blue on top. The gray undersides have orange and black spots. The Karner blue lives in northern Indiana in grassy areas near patches of oak trees. The females lay eggs on wild lupine, the only plant the caterpillars of this species eat. By thinning trees to make way for more prairie plants and planting lupine, environmentalists are working to restore the Karner blue's habitat.

10 KEY PLANTS AND ANIMALS

1. Big Bluestem Grass

Big bluestem grass is one of the grasses of the tallgrass prairie. The stems can grow higher than 6 feet (2 m), and the narrow leaves can be 2 feet (0.6 m) long. In late fall and winter when there is frost, the leaves turn reddish bronze.

2. Box Turtle

Box turtles have high-domed shells, which can have different patterns. When threatened, these turtles pull their head, legs, and tail completely inside their shell. Box turtles live on the forest floor where it is cool and damp.

3. Eastern Kingbird

The eastern kingbird is a big-shouldered gray bird with a white tip on the tail. They protect their territory and harass trespassing crows, herons, and hawks. They make sharp buzzing sounds and perch on trees and fences waiting for insects.

4. Fox Squirrel

Fox squirrels live in forests close to open landscapes. They weave twigs and leaves to make nests in old woodpecker holes. Fox squirrels eat acorns, hickory nuts, corn, and beechnuts, and they bury surplus for later.

5. Hickory

Several types of hickory trees grow throughout Indiana. Hickory trees produce hard-shelled nuts. Animals such as squirrels bury the nuts, which eventually sprout if left in the ground. In autumn, the leaves of the hickory turn yellow.

Box Turtle

Eastern Kingbird

Fox Squirrel

6. Indiana Bat

In winter, groups of the rare Indiana bat hibernate in caves in southern Indiana. In spring, they migrate to wooded areas near streams and rivers. They roost and raise their young under pieces of bark. At night, they feed on insects.

7. Long-Tailed Weasel

Long-tailed weasels hunt day and night for mice, squirrels, chipmunks, hares, frogs, snakes, and birds, using their sharp teeth. They must eat about 30 percent of their body weight each day.

8. Purple Coneflower

Purple coneflower is well known by its scientific name, *Echinacea*. A perennial plant found in meadows and fields, it has purple flowers growing on a tall stem. The flowers are used for herbal tea and an extract to treat colds and flu.

9. Robin

At sunrise, robins are the first birds to sing. In warm weather, they feed on earthworms. As fall approaches, they comb shrubs for berries. Most robins migrate south for the winter, but some stay all year if there is enough food.

10. White-Tailed Deer

White-tailed deer live in forests near meadows and fields. Their fur is red-brown in summer and gray in winter, while their bellies remain white. They stand about 3 feet (0.9 m) at the shoulder and weigh 150 to 300 pounds (68 to 136 kg).

Indiana Bat

Long-Tailed Weasel

White-Tailed Deer

CONQUEST OF THE WEST

CONQUEST

THE SITE OF
FORT SACKVILLE
CAPTURED FROM THE BRITISH
BY GEORGE ROGERS CLARK
AND HIS HEROIC COMRADES
FEBRUARY 25, 1779

The George Rogers Clark Memorial in Vincennes commemorates the fall of Fort Sackville on February 25, 1779. The surrender of the British brought the territory north of the Ohio River under the control of the United States.

From the Beginning

People have been living in the area that became the state of Indiana for at least twelve thousand years. The people who lived in this area between 8000 BCE and about 1000 or 750 BCE are of the Archaic tradition, a term that historians and scientists have used to describe the ancient people of that time. One sign of where they lived are huge piles of mussel shells left beside some of the region's streams during the later portions of the Archaic period.

The next group to inhabit the area is referred to as the people of the Woodland tradition. They lived throughout the Mississippi and Ohio valleys from about 1000 or 750 BCE to about 900 CE. They built mounds of earth near their villages. The mounds were important in their ceremonies. Mounds State Park on the White River near Anderson has some of these mounds.

People of the Mississippian tradition, who lived in what is now Indiana from about 900 to 1650 CE, also built mounds. Angel Mounds, a large town that was built during the Mississippian period near the place where the Ohio and Wabash Rivers meet, was a center for government, religion, and trade for these people. Several smaller communities from the Mississippian period were clustered along the rivers close to Angel Mounds.

This map from the *Military Journal of Ebenezer Denny* shows the layout of the Native American village called Kekionga.

Recent Native American Residents

The Miami were among the Native American groups living in the 1600s across the region that includes present-day Indiana. They lived along the Saint Joseph River and in the Wabash River valley. Their principal town, which was called Kekionga, was located where the Saint Joseph and Saint Marys Rivers meet to form the Maumee River. Two groups closely related to the Miami in language and culture were the Wea and the Piankashaw. Groups such as the Lenape (also called Delaware), Shawnee, and Potawatomi moved into what is now Indiana in the 1700s.

Europeans

French traders and **missionaries**—people who brought Christianity to new areas—came to what is now Indiana in the second half of the 1600s. They pressed west and south from Canada by way of the rivers and lakes. They were eager to discover if they could make money off the land and to meet and trade with the Native people in the area. One early explorer was René-Robert Cavelier, sieur de La Salle. He explored Lake Michigan and the Saint Joseph and Kankakee Rivers during the fall of 1679 and the winter of 1680. He continued west to the Upper Mississippi River.

News that the land had abundant wildlife, especially beavers and other valuable fur-bearing animals, brought more explorers and traders to the region. Missionaries also came and settled near some Native American villages.

To have some control over the fur trade in what is now Indiana, the French built three forts. The first was built in 1717 at Ouiatenon, the principal Wea settlement. Fort Miami was built next to Kekionga in about 1722. The third fort was established on the lower Wabash River, in the

Old Residence

Treaty negotiations between tribes and the Americans required translators. Jean Baptiste Richardville was a translator, fur trader, and the last civil chief of the Miami tribe. He signed many treaties and built a treaty house that is the oldest Native American house in Indiana.

René-Robert Cavelier, sieur de La Salle, was one of the first Europeans to see the region that is now Indiana.

area inhabited by the Piankashaw, in about 1732. Called Vincennes, this third fort grew into what is today the oldest town in Indiana.

Beginning in the late 1600s and during the 1700s, France and England (which became Great Britain in 1707) fought a series of wars with each other. The last of these wars—which in North America was called the French and Indian War—began in 1754. When the war ended in 1763, Great Britain had won. As a result, almost all the land that France had controlled in eastern North America, including what would become Indiana, passed from France to Britain.

That same year, Britain's King George III proclaimed that the land west of the Appalachian Mountains was to be reserved for Native Americans. People in Britain's American colonies along the Eastern Seaboard wanted to move west and settle this land. The British government, however, wanted to keep good relations with the Native Americans in order to avoid war and protect the fur trade. Despite the proclamation, some American colonists did settle in the Ohio and Wabash River valleys.

A New Nation

By the 1770s, many people in Britain's American colonies wanted to be free of British rule. In 1775, fighting began between colonists and British troops, and in 1776, the thirteen colonies that would form the United States declared their independence from Britain. After years of hard fighting, the colonists won the American Revolution. Under the Treaty of Paris of 1783, which officially ended the war, Great Britain recognized American independence, and it agreed to give to the new United States all British land east of the Mississippi River, south of what is now Canada, and north of Florida. In 1787, Congress passed the Northwest Ordinance, which established the Northwest Territory. It consisted of all US land north of the Ohio River and east of the Mississippi River. Nearly twenty years later, the state of Indiana would be carved from this territory.

The Native People

The largest Native tribes in Indiana were the Illinois and the Miami Confederacy, which included the Miami, Wea, Piankashaw, and Eel River tribes. In the 1700s, neighboring tribes attacked and drove out many members of the Illinois tribe. Also during that time, the Miami people suffered a series of malaria epidemics, which made way for the Kickapoo tribe to claim some of their territory.

The tribes shared the bounty of the region. They hunted deer, elk, birds, and small animals. They fished the lakes and rivers using dugout canoes. In summer, the people planted corn and vegetables. In cold weather, some groups set up camp near winter hunting grounds. In spring, people collected maple syrup, and in summer they gathered nuts, such as hickory nuts, and berries, such as huckleberries.

The Miami tribe was the largest tribe in Indiana, and they were allies of the French traders until the French lost to the British in the French and Indian War. Miami leaders distrusted the British, but they fought with them against the colonists in the Revolutionary War. As the new Americans began expanding into Indiana, they pushed the Native people out. Most tribes signed treaties with the Americans, selling their land for little and agreeing to be "removed" to other areas. The Miami held out longer. Soon the population of the Miami declined, however, as diseases such as smallpox ravaged villages. The newcomers carried germs that the Native people fell victim to because they had no immunity to foreign diseases. However, Chief Little Turtle of the Miami declared that the worst plague the Americans brought was whiskey. He said whiskey killed more of his people than all the disease and battles combined.

By 1840, the Miami people had suffered through war, disease, and loss of their ancestral land. About half of the remaining Miami people had been removed to present-day Kansas and Oklahoma. In the Treaty of the Forks of the Wabash, the remaining Miami people sold the last of their land. There are no federally recognized tribes in Indiana, although the Pokagon Band of Potawatomi Indians, Michigan and Indiana, are headquartered just north of the Indiana border in Michigan.

Spotlight on The Miami

Language: The Miami people call themselves Myaamia, meaning "Downstream People." The Miami and the Illinois people belonged to the Algonquian language group and spoke the same dialect with different accents.

The Miami built their oval homes out of reeds and wood.

Distribution: By 1846, most Miami tribal members had left Indiana for Kansas or Oklahoma, and most now live in Oklahoma, where they are a federally recognized tribe. In 1897, the population of the Miami people in Indiana had fallen so low that the federal government revoked their official status. Today, there are about four thousand members of the Miami tribe in Indiana.

Homes: The vast forests and marshlands provided the people with building materials such as reeds and wood. They wove reeds into oval-shaped dwellings and formed villages. Cornfields surrounded their communities. They also built large wooden buildings for public gatherings.

Clothing: Women wore skirts and leggings and men wore breechcloths, and all wore leather moccasins. Men shaved the sides and back of their head, keeping only the hair on the top. Women wore their hair long, braided, or tied into a bun. On certain occasions, all painted their faces. Some also had tattoos.

Food: Women planted gardens of corn, squash, and other vegetables; collected maple syrup; and foraged for nuts, seeds, roots, grasses, and berries. Men fished and hunted deer, hare, and birds such as ducks.

Crafts: The Miami wove reed and grass baskets and mats and are noted for beadwork, quillwork, and embroidery. Hunters and warriors fashioned bows and arrows, spears, and tomahawks. They carved dugout canoes from logs.

Tecumseh and William Henry Harrison came close to fighting at a meeting in 1810 to discuss the use of Native American land in what is now Indiana.

New Family

Frances Slocum was a five-year-old white girl captured in 1783 by Lenape warriors and traded to the Miami tribe. She grew up in a Native American community and married a tribal chief. When a brother and sister tracked her down and encouraged her to return with them, she refused.

In 1800, Congress created the Indiana Territory out of the Northwest Territory. Its capital was at Vincennes. Future US president William Henry Harrison was appointed governor of the new territory. He made several treaties with Native American groups, in which the Native Americans gave up large amounts of land. These treaties forced some Native Americans to move, some as far west as present-day Kansas and Oklahoma.

Tecumseh, a leader of the Shawnee people, rallied many Native Americans to oppose the white people who were settling on Native American traditional land. He said that this land belonged to all Native Americans and that individual bands did not have the right to sell or grant land to the whites. His followers gathered at the junction of the Tippecanoe and Wabash Rivers.

Governor Harrison did not like the idea that Native Americans might be preparing for war against the white people. So, on November 7, 1811, Harrison led an army against the Shawnee in what would be called the Battle of Tippecanoe. The Native Americans were defeated.

Tecumseh, however, worked to rebuild his forces. Meanwhile, the United States and Britain clashed in what is known as the War of 1812. Tecumseh sided with the British. Harrison was named commander of the US Army of the Northwest, and in 1813, he defeated British and Native American forces. Tecumseh was killed in that battle. The war with Britain ended in 1815. Most Native Americans who remained in the Indiana Territory were soon forced out.

A New State

As more white settlers came to the Indiana Territory, it was divided into smaller units. The Michigan Territory was created in 1805 and the Illinois Territory in 1809. In 1813, Corydon was named the capital of the Indiana Territory. In the summer of 1816, delegates met to write a state constitution. On August 15 of that same year, Jonathan Jennings, Indiana's representative in Congress, was elected governor. A few months later, on December 11, 1816, Indiana became the nineteenth US state.

Visitors can learn about life in the early nineteenth century at the historic site of the town of New Harmony.

Making a Woven Basket

With a never-ending supply of reeds and grasses, the Native people of Indiana wove useful and quite beautiful grass baskets. Many traded their baskets to western tribes for bison hides.

What You Need

Paintbrush

Brown paint

Friendship bracelet cords

15 to 21 craft sticks

Paper cup

Scissors

Craft glue

What To Do

- Cut the top off of a paper cup, leave about a 2-inch (5 cm) "wall" around the bottom of the cup.
- Glue wooden craft sticks to the wall of the paper cup, leaving a small space between each one.
- The number of craft sticks that fit around the cup will vary depending on the size of the cup. Be sure to use an odd number of craft sticks.
- Paint the outside of your basket and let it dry.
- To begin weaving the bracelet cord, tie an end around a stick and slide it down until it touches the top of the wall of the paper cup.

- Weave the cord, over and under.
- To change colors, tie the next color cord to the last color. Snip extra cord.
- Tuck the knot behind the craft sticks.
- Continue as long as you like.
- When finished, cut cord and glue the end to a craft stick.

After Indiana became a state, more people moved to the area. Many of these pioneers came to the state by way of the Ohio River. They came from Kentucky, Virginia, North Carolina, Pennsylvania, New York, and elsewhere. The Indiana constitution of 1816 barred slavery, but it did not clearly state whether existing slaves had to be freed. Some white settlers brought their slaves with them to Indiana.

The land these new arrivals entered was densely wooded. It could take years for a farm family to clear the land of all the trees and stumps. Once it was cleared, however, the land served the farmers well. As soon as a field was clear enough to be planted, corn, hay, potatoes, and flax were among the first crops to go in. Corn was a nutritious food, for both the family and their livestock. Flax was woven into cloth. Settlers logged trees to build log cabins, fences, boats, and wagons. Wood was also used for fuel for cooking and heating.

Growth and Removal

Abraham Lincoln's family was among the early settlers who came from Kentucky. Lincoln was seven years old when his father took the family across the Ohio River into Indiana. The Lincolns arrived in 1816 and stayed for fourteen years before moving to Illinois. Like many other Indiana families, the Lincolns lived on a large tract of land—about 160 acres (65 ha). Only a small portion of the land was cleared and farmed, however.

A young Abraham Lincoln lived on this homestead in Indiana with his family before they moved to Illinois.

Carriages that traveled the early roads of Indiana can be seen at the Alton Goin Historical Museum.

During early statehood, although most Native Americans had already left the area, a few groups still remained in Indiana. However, treaties that were negotiated with the Wea, Miami, Lenape, and Potawatomi in 1818 took away more of their land or required them to move farther west. The Potawatomi were forced to leave in 1838, and the Miami finally surrendered the last parcel of tribal land in Indiana in 1846. The practice of negotiating for land at a cheap price in exchange for Native Americans leaving the state was called the "Indian Removals."

In 1820, the state legislature decided to build a new capital. The following year, it approved a recommendation that the capital be located at the geographic center of the state. The lawmakers chose to call this place Indianapolis. The state government moved to Indianapolis in 1825.

Transportation and Improvements

Transportation was of great concern to the new state. People wanted a dependable way to move goods to markets in the eastern and southern states. Building a network of roads, canals, and railroads seemed to be the answer. In 1826, the legislature decided to build a north-south highway through the state. This would be called the Michigan Road. The east-west National Road, a project begun by the federal government, was extended across Indiana from 1827 to 1834. It was used by wagons that carried people and goods between Maryland in the east and Illinois in the west. (The Michigan Road's route is now covered by several different highways. The National Road is now US Highway 40.)

In 1836, the legislature passed the Mammoth Internal Improvements Act. The act provided $10 million to be used to build canals and rail lines and to improve the roads. Only small sections of the canals were built at that time. It would not be until 1853 that the Wabash and Erie Canal, which went from Lake Erie to Fort Wayne and then south to Evansville, would be completed. By then, canals were not as useful as they might have

Quaker Levi Coffin helped many former slaves gain their freedom by moving them along the Underground Railroad.

been twenty years earlier, however. By the 1850s, railroads had become the preferred means of long-distance travel.

Slavery and the Civil War

Although slavery was officially barred in Indiana, many Indianans were not opposed to slavery. Many believed, for example, that there was nothing wrong with white people enslaving Africans in the Southern states or even in the new territories and states being created farther west as the United States grew. The legislature passed laws that were meant to prevent or to at least discourage free blacks (African Americans who had never been enslaved or had been legally freed from slavery) from settling in Indiana. Few Indianans believed that slavery should be abolished (ended) nationwide.

Nevertheless, the Underground Railroad did have routes through Indiana. This was not an actual railway. It was a network of people who helped and sheltered people escaping slavery to flee to states that prohibited slavery or to Canada and other countries. The journey was risky for the escapees as well as for their guides and protectors. The town of Newport (now called Fountain City) was a "station," or stopping place, on the Underground Railroad. Many of the escaped people found shelter there in the home of Levi and Catharine Coffin, who were Quakers. They helped more than two thousand runaway slaves escape to freedom.

Meanwhile, in 1851, voters in Indiana approved a new state constitution. Article XIII of the constitution included harsh rules regarding African Americans. It made it illegal for African Americans to come into or to settle in Indiana. It prohibited anyone from giving a job to an African American.

In Their Own Words

"The Bible, in bidding us to feed the hungry and clothe the naked, said nothing about color, and I should try to follow out the teachings of that good book."
—Levi Coffin, Indiana Quaker, abolitionist, and so-called president of the Underground Railroad

★ 10 KEY CITIES ★

Indianapolis

South Bend

1. Indianapolis: population 820,445

Indianapolis is the second-largest city in the Midwest after Chicago. Established in 1821, it is a center for business, culture, sports, and entertainment. Called the Crossroads of America, the city is a junction for several US highways.

2. Fort Wayne: population 253,691

Fort Wayne was established as a fort in 1794 at the **confluence** of the St. Joseph, St. Marys, and Maumee Rivers. After the Wabash and Erie Canal was built, the city became a hub for industry, transportation, and shipping.

3. Evansville: population 117,429

White settlers incorporated the city in 1817. It soon became a trading center for river boats and the railroad. It has a thriving economy and is home to the University of Southern Indiana.

4. South Bend: population 101,168

Lying along the southern bend of the St. Joseph River, South Bend is the hub of northern Indiana. Suffering job losses during the latest recession, the city is now attracting new technology employers. South Bend is the home of the University of Notre Dame.

5. Hammond: population 80,830

Hammond is a suburb of Chicago. Of particular interest to visitors is the John Dillinger Museum. Dillinger, a criminal in the early part of the twentieth century, was the first person to be declared by the FBI as "Public Enemy Number One."

INDIANA ★ ★ ★ ★

6. Bloomington: population 80,405

Bloomington, named by settlers for its natural beauty, is the home of Indiana University. It is one of the highest ranked schools in the country. Notable graduates include Nobel Prize winners and world leaders.

7. Gary: population 80,294

Gary borders Lake Michigan and is near the Indiana Dunes National Lakeshore. Founded by the United States Steel Corporation in 1906, Gary flourished for decades before declining. Gary is built on high quality sand once mined to make glass.

8. Carmel: population 79,191

Carmel is a popular suburb of Indianapolis. It is often cited as one of the country's most livable cities. The city features a thriving arts and crafts district, featuring hand blown glass. Glassmaking was one of Indiana's early industries.

9. Fishers: population 76,794

Fishers, once called "Fishers Switch," is a fast growing suburb of Indianapolis. It is known for its safety, good schools, and environmental awareness. There are many festivals and concerts in the city, among them the Fishers Freedom Festival.

10. Muncie: population 70,085

Muncie is home to Ball State University, named for the five Ball brothers who moved their glass business to Muncie from Buffalo, New York, in the nineteenth century. Glass sculpture is arrayed throughout the city.

Bloomington

Muncie

In addition, any legal agreements made with African Americans would be considered worthless. In 1866, the Indiana Supreme Court declared Article XIII null and void, which means it was invalid. This article was officially repealed in 1881.

Studebaker Brand

During the Civil War, Clement Studebaker made wagons for the army, and afterward, he made wagons used by pioneers along the Oregon Trail. In 1902, he made his first electric car, and in 1912, his first gas-powered car. The last Studebaker automobile to roll off the assembly line in South Bend was in 1966.

Even before the Civil War began in 1861, Indianans debated whether the Southern states should be permitted to secede, or separate, from the Union (another name commonly used for the United States at that time). In the months after Abraham Lincoln was elected president in November 1860, eleven Southern states did secede, forming the Confederate States of America. Lincoln was personally opposed to slavery, and many white Southerners believed the future of slavery in the United States was threatened by his election. Many Hoosiers sympathized with the

Manufacturing became a major part of the state economy in the late 1800s. These women are making toys in the mid-twentieth century.

The Inland Steel Company began producing steel in Indiana more than a century ago.

Southern states. However, Oliver Morton, who was governor from 1861 to 1867, believed the Union should be preserved. So, during the Civil War, Indiana stayed in the Union, and it sent men to fight on the Union (or Northern) side. There was little actual fighting in the state during the Civil War. Only one Civil War battle was fought in Indiana, near Corydon, and the Union lost to the Confederate army. After four years of bloody fighting elsewhere, the South was defeated in 1865, the Southern states eventually returned to the Union, and the Thirteenth Amendment to the US Constitution was adopted, abolishing slavery throughout the United States.

Leading to the Twentieth Century

By the 1860s, the landscape of Indiana was greatly changed from what it had been at the beginning of the century. About one-half of the forests had been cleared. Roads, railroads, and waterways made it easier for people to come to Indiana or for Indianans to travel or ship goods to other states.

During this time, most Hoosiers still lived on farms, but small towns were growing. There were many new mills and factories using the resources of Indiana to manufacture a great variety of industrial and household products. With the end of the Civil War, immigration from the South to Indiana was renewed. The population, once concentrated in the southern half of the state, began to spread northward.

The Grange, a social and educational organization for farm families, came to Indiana in 1869. Grange members joined together and formed cooperatives. This allowed them to bargain for more favorable shipping rates for their farm products. The Grange also asked state legislators for better tax rates and to have mail delivered to addresses in rural areas.

Laborers in Indiana's factories became active in labor unions. These organizations brought workers together so they could bargain with factory owners for better wages and working conditions. The Knights of Labor, a group that fought for workers' rights, gained many members in the early 1880s. It allowed women to be members and worked to get approval of an eight-hour workday, instead of the ten-hour or twelve-hour days that were customary at the time.

Natural gas was discovered in northern Indiana in 1867. Twenty years later, gas wells tapped this fuel so that it could be used. Many people thought the gas supply would last forever. Anyone who opened a factory could use the gas for free. This free gas led to Kokomo and Anderson being transformed into manufacturing towns. Muncie, called the City of Eternal Gas, was known for glassmaking and for steel, nail, and wire production. By the start of the twentieth century, however, the gas was pretty much used up, and the industrial boom fizzled out.

Progress continued in Indiana, however. For instance, Elwood Haynes test-drove a self-propelled, gasoline-powered vehicle on the roads outside Kokomo on July 4, 1894. Within a few years, Indiana had hundreds of companies building cars and making car parts. Studebaker, which had started in 1852 as a blacksmith shop and wagonmaker, began to make electric cars in 1902. Then, in 1904, the company started making gasoline-powered cars. Cars changed how people spent their leisure time. At the end of the nineteenth century, Indiana was a leading center for car manufacturing in the United States. Michigan came to dominate the automobile industry, but in 1909, Indiana still ranked second, producing about 13 percent of the country's automobiles, compared to Michigan's 51 percent.

In the late 1800s and early 1900s, the Calumet region, east of Chicago, developed into one of the nation's most important industrial centers. The Standard Oil Company began building an enormous oil refinery at Whiting in 1889, to make gasoline and other products from crude oil. It went into operation the following year. Inland Steel started constructing a steel mill at East Chicago, Indiana, in 1901.

In 1905, the United States Steel Corporation bought 9,000 acres (3,642 ha) of land on the shore of Lake Michigan. It had plans to level the sand dunes and to build the world's largest steel mill. It would also build a town, to be named Gary. Rail lines and harbors already served the region, and numerous large and small mills and factories opened in Calumet. People heard there were jobs to be had at US Steel and other companies, and they came to Indiana to work. Many of them came from as far away as Eastern Europe, from Poland, Hungary, Slovakia, and Czechoslovakia.

Challenging Times

At the turn of the twentieth century, society was facing many challenges. For instance, a branch of the Ku Klux Klan (also referred to as the KKK) was set up in Evansville, Indiana, in 1920. The KKK, started in the South after the Civil War, was an organization that was against African Americans as well as Jews and Roman Catholics. Membership in the Klan grew to 250,000 people in Indiana in the early 1920s. In the 1924 elections, the influence of the Klan helped the governor, a majority of state legislators, and several city mayors to win office. The power of the Klan in Indiana crumbled after its leader in

A member of the Ku Klux Klan, which gained a foothold in Indiana in 1920, seeks support during a 1972 demonstration in Columbus.

the state, D. C. Stephenson, was convicted of murder in 1925. Some Klan activity continued, however, in subsequent decades.

Other problems came to Indiana beginning in the late 1920s. The Great Depression, which started in 1929, hit Indiana hard. During this time of severe economic hardship, prices for farm products dropped and factories closed or cut back on their operations. By 1933, about one-quarter of workers in the state were out of work. In some towns, unemployment was much higher. In southern Indiana, the flooding of the Ohio River in 1937 added to the region's difficulties.

During this time, African Americans were faced with even more challenges. Indiana had separate schools for white and black students. Segregated schools remained legal in Indiana until 1949. This often meant that African-American children attended poorer schools that were not equipped with materials that white students had. Desegregation laws—which were designed to make things equal for African Americans and whites—went into effect, but some school districts disregarded them. It would take many more decades for some schools to arrange to have black and white students together.

New Growth

The middle of the twentieth century brought new prosperity to Indiana. During World War II, Indiana's economy bounced back. Fighting had begun in Europe in 1939, and the United States entered the war in 1941. Farms and industries, especially steel, helped to supply the war effort. Then, after World War II ended in 1945, manufacturers turned their attention to making consumer goods. For instance, things such as refrigerators were made in Evansville. So many refrigerators were made there that Evansville for a while was known as the refrigerator capital.

During the 1950s, many people began to buy houses in the suburbs around Indiana's larger cities. Many small stores in the downtown areas of large cities closed their doors and moved to the new shopping malls, which were often located in the suburbs. This made the downtown areas of large cities look empty and worn out. Then, in the 1960s, to correct this problem, the federal government provided money and support for urban

A tornado outbreak in 2013 caused widespread damage in Indiana. This dog rests outside a former home in Boonville.

Pilot Program

Women Airforce Service Pilots [WASPs] were trained during World War II to support the military while male pilots fought overseas. As a WASP, Fort Wayne's Margaret Ray Ringenberg flew transport planes and trained combat pilots. She continued flying and racing after the war, finishing in third place in her last race, at age eighty-seven.

renewal projects. These projects helped cities such as Indianapolis and Gary to benefit from the creation of new housing and business districts, as well as civic, cultural, and recreational facilities.

In the following decades, Indiana weathered cycles of economic good times and bad times. Some businesses and industries failed while others flourished. Many people from across the country and around the world moved to the state. By 1999, Indiana's population rose past six million.

Meanwhile, natural disasters occasionally tested Indiana residents. A particularly deadly tornado outbreak struck central and northern areas of the state on April 11, 1965. In a tornado outbreak, one weather system creates many tornadoes. That day, which happened to be Palm Sunday, 137 people were killed as eleven tornadoes hit twenty counties. A record thirty-seven

A new terminal brought Indianapolis International Airport into the twenty-first century.

Medal Haul

In the 1972 Olympic Games in Munich, Germany, Indiana University swimmer Mark Spitz won seven gold medals. That record for most gold medals won at one Olympics stood until 2008, when Michael Phelps won eight gold medals in Beijing.

tornadoes tore through thirty-one counties on June 2, 1990. In June 2008, record flooding caused damage estimated at more than $1 billion in central and southern areas of the state. One of the largest tornado outbreaks ever struck the Midwest on November 17, 2013. That day, thirty tornadoes struck Indiana, and dozens of others caused havoc in other states.

Through it all, residents of Indiana remained strong and continued to work toward making their state the best it could be. Toward the end of the 1990s, for example, Indianapolis's public facilities began to see one upgrade after another. A new arena for the city's pro basketball teams opened in 1999. This was followed by major expansions of the Indianapolis Museum of Art and the Eiteljorg Museum of American Indians and Western Art, a new billion-dollar international air terminal, a new retractable-roof football stadium, and reconstruction of the Interstate 495 bypass on the west side of the city. During the recessions of the early twenty-first century, Indiana weathered and recovered better than many other parts of the country. In June 2015, the unemployment rate was 4.8 percent in Indiana and 5.3 percent in the US.

10 KEY DATES IN STATE HISTORY

1. 10,000 BCE

Ancient nomadic people live in the region that will include present-day Indiana. They were hunters and gatherers who foraged and followed mammoths and bison.

2. 1100-1450 BCE

The present-day Angel Mounds area is a trade, political, cultural, and religious center for ancestors of today's Native Americans. They mysteriously disappeared.

3. 1732

French traders, who had friendly relations with the Miami tribe, made their first permanent settlement in Vincennes, in what is now Indiana.

4. September 3, 1783

The American Revolution ends. Land that includes present-day Indiana becomes part of the United States. The Siege of Sackville near Vincennes had ousted the British from Indiana in 1779.

5. July 13, 1787

The Northwest Territory, which includes Indiana, is formed. Laws prohibit slavery, promote education, and guarantee religious freedom and civil rights.

6. December 11, 1816

Delegates draft a constitution, and with more than the required number of sixty thousand residents, Indiana, becomes the nineteenth state.

7. June 5, 1909

The Indianapolis Motor Speedway opens with balloon races. The first automobile race takes place later that year, on August 19. The first official Indy 500 is held in 1911.

8. March 29, 1984

The National Football League's Baltimore Colts move to Indianapolis and become the Indianapolis Colts. The team is the host for the annual football scouting combine.

9. April 2, 2006

For the first time since 1970, most Indiana counties begin observing daylight saving time. However, the state remains inconveniently divided between eastern and central time zones.

10. April 2, 2015

The Indiana legislature amends a controversial religious freedom law after national outcries from citizens who feared the law could lead to discrimination.

The Amish, such as this woman making egg noodles
in Middlebury, have long been residents of Indiana.

The People

The people of Indiana are a mix of long-time Hoosiers and newer residents who have moved there for jobs or a more relaxed way of life. They represent the variety of histories and heritages that have come together in Indiana.

In 1800, when the US Congress split up the huge Northwest Territory, the western portion, where far more Native Americans than whites lived at the time, became a new territory that was given the name Indiana. The name means "land of the Indians." When states were eventually formed from this territory, one of them kept the name Indiana.

Most people in Indiana belong to families who have lived in the state for more than a generation. About 68 percent of Indiana's people were born in the state, and nearly everyone—96 percent—was born in the United States. Hoosiers are very proud of their state, and very proud to call themselves Hoosiers. Where the name came from is anybody's guess, and there have been many guesses.

The nickname was already popular in the 1830s, when it began to appear in print. Many people have tried to explain the origin of the word. One idea is that it was brought to the region by settlers from areas of the South where people who lived in the hills used to be called "hoosiers," from an old English word for hill. Another theory suggests that Indiana river men were so good at beating, or "hushing," their opponents in fights that they became known as "hushers," which eventually became "hoosiers." Yet another theory is that a man called Hoosier used to hire workers from Indiana for the Louisville and Portland Canal, and these people came to be known as "Hoosier's men." These are only some of the explanations that have been proposed. None is completely convincing.

Cities and Towns

Indiana has only a handful of midsized cities. Many Hoosiers live in small towns or in the suburbs around the bigger cities. The population of Indiana today is concentrated in the middle and in the north of the state. Marion County, in the center of the state, has the highest population. It contains Indianapolis, the state's capital and largest city.

Lake County, in northern Indiana east of Chicago, is the second-largest county in terms of population. The city of Gary is in Lake County. Allen County, also in the north, is the third-largest county. Fort Wayne, the second-largest city in Indiana, is located in Allen County. Evansville, in southern Indiana, is the third-largest city. Other sizable cities and towns are South Bend, Hammond, Bloomington, Fishers, Carmel, and Muncie. Many of Indiana's smaller towns have only a few hundred to a few thousand residents.

A passion for basketball is instilled early in Indiana.

Ethnic and Racial Groups

In Indiana, about 84 percent of the population is white, and many of them are of a European heritage. Immigrants to Indiana came as laborers, skilled workers, farmers, servants, business people, and professional people, such as lawyers or doctors. They came for many reasons: to escape religious persecution, prejudice, or poverty. Others came just because they had a spirit of adventure.

In the mid-1800s, in addition to farming, mining, and working on the canals or railroads, textile manufacturing was a booming business and a great allure for those wanting to start a new life. By 1860, there were seventy-nine woolen mills and two cotton mills in

The town of Lyles Station was founded in the 1840s by African Americans from Tennessee.

Engine Exposed

The international tractor manufacturer Cummins has a museum in its headquarters featuring antique cars and racecars. However, many people come to see a giant sculpture of an "exploded" diesel engine. The sculptor suspended every part of a massive replica of a diesel engine by wires to show how they all fit together.

operation in Indiana. There were simply not enough native Indianans to run the looms. Owners of mills sent out "broadsheets," which were flyers encouraging people to come to Indiana and work in the mills. The call was answered by many German, Irish, English, and Scottish immigrants.

At the end of the 1800s and in the early 1900s, people from Poland, Czechoslovakia, Hungary, Serbia, Croatia, and other Eastern European countries migrated to Indiana to work in the steel mills and other industries. People from Greece and Italy were also attracted to life in Indiana. Many came to work in the mines.

African Americans make up about 9 percent of the population in Indiana. Many African Americans in Indiana are descended from people who moved to the state from the South. During the first half of the 1800s, African Americans who came to Indiana

★ 10 ★ KEY PEOPLE ★ ★

Jim Davis

Michael Jackson

David Letterman

1. Johnny Appleseed

John Chapman, born in Massachusetts, moved west and planted an apple orchard in Fort Wayne. His mission was to provide healthy food for pioneers. He gave away trees and apple seeds, or sold them for just pennies.

2. Joshua Bell

Bloomington-born Joshua Bell is a classical violinist who performed at New York City's Carnegie Hall at age eighteen. An award-winning director of St. Martin of the Fields Orchestra, he tours, records, and produces TV specials.

3. Jim Davis

Jim Davis grew up on a farm in Marion. He had asthma and spent hours indoors, drawing. After graduating with an art degree, he drew cartoons. His second character, a sassy, fat, lazy, lasagna-eating cat named Garfield, is read by millions each day.

4. The Jackson 5

The Jackson 5 was a family of musicians from Gary who were signed by Motown Records in 1969 when the youngest, Michael, was only eleven. They performed on television and sold out concert venues. Michael Jackson went on to a very successful solo career, as did his sister Janet, who was born in 1966.

5. David Letterman

David Letterman was born in Indianapolis. He studied radio and television at Ball State University, and served as the host for late night talk shows for a record thirty years. He won many Emmy Awards before retiring in 2015.

INDIANA ★ ★ ★ ★

6. Jane Pauley

Television journalist Margaret Jane Pauley, born in Indianapolis, began her career at WISH-TV in Indianapolis. She went on to become a correspondent for *NBC Today*, *Dateline*, and the *NBC Nightly News*. She has received an Emmy Award.

Jane Pauley

7. Orville Redenbacher

Orville Redenbacher, born in Brazil, Indiana, graduated from Purdue University with a degree in agronomy. He developed a popcorn that bears his name and appeared in TV commercials to sell it.

8. Oscar Robertson

Oscar Robertson grew up in Indianapolis. A star guard at the University of Cincinnati, he won an Olympic basketball gold medal in 1960, a National Basketball Association title in 1971, and set assist records. He was inducted into the Basketball Hall of Fame in 1980.

Madame C. J. Walker

9. Madame C. J. Walker

Sarah Breedlove was orphaned young. When she moved to Indianapolis with her third husband, she changed her name to Madame C. J. Walker. In 1905, she invented hair care products for African-American women. They made her America's first female self-made millionaire.

Kurt Vonnegut

10. Kurt Vonnegut

Kurt Vonnegut is a literary legend. After a childhood in Indianapolis, he was a prisoner of war during World War II, then he taught English, sold cars, and wrote stories. His first success was *Slaughterhouse-Five, or The Children's Crusade*.

Who Indianans Are

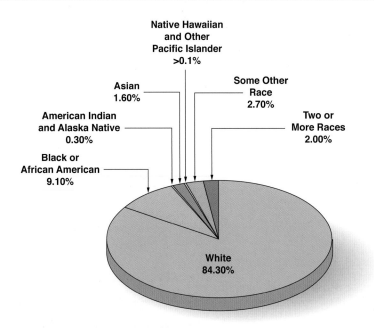

Native Hawaiian and Other Pacific Islander >0.1%

Asian 1.60%

American Indian and Alaska Native 0.30%

Some Other Race 2.70%

Black or African American 9.10%

Two or More Races 2.00%

White 84.30%

Total Population
6,483,802

Hispanic or Latino (of any race):
- 389,707 (6%)

Note: The pie chart shows the racial breakdown of the state's population based on the categories used by the US Bureau of the Census. The Census Bureau reports information for Hispanics or Latinos separately, since they may be of any race. Percentages in the pie chart may not add to 100 because of rounding.

Source: US Bureau of the Census, 2010 Census

Hogging the Track

After the 1920 Marion International Motorcycle Race, the winners, who rode Harley Davidson motorcycles, circled the track with pigs on their laps in celebration. The riders began calling their Harleys "hogs," and the name stuck. Winners of the race still do victory laps with pigs.

had been enslaved, or had escaped from slavery. Other African Americans who were no longer enslaved chose Indiana because slavery in the Northwest Territory and in the state was illegal.

After the abolition of slavery in the United States in 1865, African Americans left the South and came to Indiana so they could buy land or find work in the many new factories. After World War I, more African Americans moved to Indiana, lured by many new job opportunities in manufacturing. The Calumet region was a popular destination. Today, the black population is greatest in Indiana's industrial counties and cities. The population of both Marion County and Lake County is about 26 percent African American. The city of Gary's population is roughly four-fifths African American.

In many towns and cities, people celebrate Juneteenth, the holiday marking the day that the last enslaved Africans in America learned that they were free, more than two years after the Emancipation Proclamation was issued in 1863. The holiday is celebrated

Asian Americans contribute to cultural diversity in Indiana.

with large picnics, music, dance, and speeches. It is a time for all races and ethnicities to celebrate the African-American heritage of Indiana.

About 1 percent of the population is Asian American. Most Asian Americans live in the larger cities and in the university towns of West Lafayette and Bloomington. Native Alaskans, Native Hawaiians and other Pacific Islanders, and Native Americans make up less than one percent of the population in Indiana. The Miami tribe has its tribal headquarters in Peru. Among its activities is an annual Native American Powwow.

Hispanics

When answering questions from the US Census Bureau, people may identify themselves as being Hispanic or Latino. They or their families are from a Spanish-speaking nation or culture. People who are Hispanic or Latino may be of any race.

Many people from Mexico moved to the Calumet region of Indiana in the 1920s. Some found jobs with railroad companies. Others worked in the steel mills there.

The overall population in Indiana has increased nearly seven percent in the past few years. Of that seven percent, more than 40 percent of growth has been due to increases in the Hispanic population. Although Indiana has a lower percentage of Hispanic residents than the national average, the state's Hispanic or Latino population is nonetheless growing rapidly. Most of the people of Hispanic heritage in Indiana are from Mexico. Others are from Puerto Rico, Cuba, and countries in Central America. Most of the state's Hispanic population is centered in the largest cities and suburbs in Lake and Marion Counties. Job and educational opportunities are changing, however, and more Hispanic families are moving to smaller cities and towns. Since 1968, when President Lyndon Johnson declared National Hispanic Heritage Week (President Ronald Reagan later extended it to a month), many Indiana communities have celebrated their Hispanic friends and neighbors.

Population Changes

In general, the population of Indiana is gradually increasing. This growth is due mainly to what is called natural increase, which means that there are more births than deaths. Also, new residents are coming to Indiana from other states and other countries, seeking the kind of quality of life Indiana offers.

Despite the overall trend of a slowly increasing population, in some recent years there have been more people moving out of the state than people moving from elsewhere into Indiana. The people who move away are often young and college educated. Indiana's business and education leaders worry about the effect this loss of skilled people has on Indiana's economy. They are working to create research centers and companies to make Indiana attractive to these talented young people, as well as to other people who may want to come live in the state.

Education

The first school in the state was run by a Catholic priest in Vincennes in 1793. As new settlers arrived, their fear of wild animals and battles between the French, the British, and Native tribes convinced them to keep their children home. Frontier life did not leave much room for home-schooling, so teachers went to people's homes. After Native Americans and the settlers learned to live in peace, settlers converted small army blockhouses into schoolhouses. There were few books or school supplies, but Indianans valued education, so the government made an effort to fund public education for all.

Today, Indiana has 407 school districts serving more than one million preschool through high school students. More than 87 percent of Indiana students graduate, which is higher than the national rate. Students also score above the national average on national standardized tests.

Indiana has excellent colleges and universities that prepare students for careers in science, engineering, high-technology industries, education, and other businesses and professions. There are more than one hundred community colleges, private colleges, and vocational schools in Indiana. The major public universities include Indiana University, which has its main campus in Bloomington. The university has highly ranked schools of business, music, law, and computing, and it boasts one of the first departments of environmental science in the country. Indiana State University in Terre Haute was founded in 1865 as a teachers' college, and it continues its tradition by being an important Midwest research university. Purdue University, which was founded in 1869 with a grant from an Indiana businessman named John Purdue, has its main campus in West Lafayette. It was founded in part to be an engineering school and continues to attract people who want to study engineering and related fields. Purdue has one of the largest international student populations in the country. Perhaps Indiana's best-known university, Notre Dame,

High-tech medical research is done at the MED Institute in West Lafayette.

is located near South Bend. Founded in 1842 by Irish Catholic priest-educators, Notre Dame served only a handful of students in its early years. By the twenty-first century, its enrollment was close to twelve thousand students, drawn from across the United States and dozens of other countries. Notre Dame is particularly famous for its college sports programs. Student athletes are known as the Fighting Irish.

Religion

Nearly 80 percent of Indianans follow a Christian religion. Protestant denominations include Baptist, Lutheran, and Methodist, and many Protestants are Evangelicals. Of all the Christian churches, the largest single one is Roman Catholic. Other faiths include Mormonism, Judaism, Islam, and Buddhism.

The Amish

In the 1700s, a group known as the Amish began migrating to America from Europe. They were Anabaptists, a form of Christianity, who fled religious persecution. They settled in Pennsylvania and in 1841, began moving to Indiana. Indiana has the third-greatest Amish population in the world. The Amish are noted for living a nineteenth-century way of life. They dress simply in clothing of that era, including modest dresses and bonnets for women and straw hats and suspenders for men. They live without modern conveniences such as cars and electricity. Belief in family, community, and respect for nature is the heart of their life and religious faith. The Amish remain separate from the outside world and maintain their own governing councils. They produce their own food and nearly all their household needs. At age sixteen, Amish teens are allowed to leave the community to experience the wider world in order to decide if they want to live the rest of their lives in the community. Nearly 90 percent return and choose to live in the traditional Amish way. Elkhart and Lagrange Counties are the home of the largest Amish settlements.

★ 10 KEY EVENTS ★

Bill Monroe Memorial Bean Blossom Bluegrass Festival

Hoosier Hysteria

1. Bill Monroe Memorial Bean Blossom Bluegrass Festival

Banjo players, fiddlers, and singers gather at Bean Blossom in June to share their love of bluegrass music. Bill Monroe, known as the father of bluegrass, founded the festival in 1967. It is the world's oldest continuously running annual festival devoted to bluegrass.

2. Circus City Festival

Peru, home of the International Circus Hall of Fame, celebrates its heritage with a nine-day party. The festival features a circus parade with vintage wagons, clowns, and wild animals. The parade is the oldest circus parade in the country.

3. Eiteljorg Museum Indian Market and Festival

Each June, the Indianapolis Eiteljorg Museum hosts a weekend festival honoring Native American artists, craftspeople, performers, and musicians. Visitors can enjoy Native American music, food, demonstrations, and performances.

4. Ethnic Expo

Residents of Columbus are hosts each August to an international array of musicians, chefs, and artists who share their cultures and achievements with more than thirty thousand festivalgoers. The expo starts with a large parade.

5. Hoosier Hysteria

Indiana has its own version of March Madness, known as Hoosier Hysteria. In March, the top boys' and girls' high school basketball teams go to Indianapolis to play in the finals tournaments. The games draw tens of thousands of fans.

INDIANA ★ ★ ★ ★

6. Indianapolis 500

The Indianapolis 500 auto race is held at the Indianapolis Motor Speedway in May. In this world-famous race, thirty-three cars take two hundred laps to complete a 500-mile (805 km) course and at speeds topping 220 miles per hour (354 kmh).

7. Indiana State Fair

August at the state fair in Indianapolis brings in farmers who show off their best livestock and farm products. Manufacturers display their latest farm equipment. Fairgoers come for the rides and entertainment. The first fair was held in 1852.

8. Lanesville Heritage Weekend

Lanesville Heritage Weekend brings Indiana's farming roots to life. There are tractor pulls, displays of antique farm machinery, and demonstrations of traditional crafts such as quilting, blacksmithing, broom making, wood carving, and spinning.

9. Limestone Heritage Festival

Bedford citizens celebrate their limestone-mining heritage on the Fourth of July. The festival kicks off on July 3 with a barbeque cook-off. Other festivities include a pancake breakfast, live music, dancing, and fireworks.

10. Shipshewana Ice Festival

Shipshewana hosts a two-day Ice Festival at the end of December. In the town's main square, festivalgoers watch as master ice sculptors carve, shave, and drill their creations. There is also a chili cook-off.

Indianapolis 500

Indiana State Fair

City Hall is where many of the decisions affecting Muncie are made.

How the Government Works

I ndiana has had two state constitutions. The first one was written in 1816, a little before Indiana became a state. The second constitution was written in 1851, and it, along with amendments, is the present-day constitution. Indiana's state constitution lays out the functions and powers of each branch of government. There have been more than sixty constitutional changes, or amendments, made over the years. The Indiana constitution begins with a bill of rights, which is a list of basic rights guaranteed to each person in the state. The constitution goes on to describe the organization and powers of the state government.

Counties, Cities, Towns, and Townships

Indiana's ninety-two counties are made up of cities, towns, and townships. The state's legislature, called the Indiana General Assembly, decides how the local governments are to be organized. Each of the local governments has a legislative

In Their Own Words

"It is better to vote for what you want and not get it than to vote for what you don't want and get it."
—Eugene V. Debs, of Terre Haute, union leader and five-time Socialist Party presidential candidate

The governor and the legislature work in the Indiana Statehouse in Indianapolis.

and executive branch that can form rules and laws that are specific to their communities, as long as they are not in conflict with state or federal law.

In Indiana's counties (except Marion County), a three-member board of commissioners serves as the executive branch, and a seven-member county council works as the legislative body. Aside from Indianapolis, each city has a mayor and a legislative council. Towns have a town council, and the president of the town council is the executive officer. A township is led by a trustee and a township board. In 1970, Indianapolis became what is called a consolidated city. The boundaries of Indianapolis were extended to match the boundaries of Marion County, where Indianapolis is located. In addition, the city and the county governments were combined to form a new government called Unigov. The legislative body is the city-county council. The mayor and the mayor's office form the executive branch. Although Unigov covers all of Marion County, a number of excluded cities and townships in the county keep certain powers.

Indianans in Congress

Indiana is represented in the US Congress in Washington, DC. Like all states, it has two members in the US Senate. The number of members each state has in the US House of Representatives is related to the state's population. Based on the results of the 2010 US census, Indiana has nine representatives in the US House.

State Government

Like the federal government, the Indiana state government has three branches: the executive, legislative, and judicial. Each branch has its own powers and responsibilities. The executive branch is headed by the governor. The legislative branch is the lawmaking body.

Statues representing agriculture and commerce greet visitors to the statehouse.

The judicial branch consists of the courts. Indiana's schools are overseen by the state board of education. This board is headed by an elected official, the superintendent of public instruction. It has ten other members. Eight are appointed by the governor, and the other two are appointed by the speaker of the house and the president pro tem of the senate.

Branches of Government

Executive

The executive branch enforces the laws of Indiana. The governor is Indiana's chief executive. The governor and lieutenant governor are elected together to serve for a term of four years. Other elected officials in the executive branch with four-year terms include the attorney general, secretary of state, auditor, treasurer, and superintendent of public instruction. The governor, lieutenant governor, secretary of state, auditor, and treasurer cannot serve more than eight years in any twelve-year period.

Legislative

The state legislature is known as the Indiana General Assembly. It creates laws for the state. It has two houses, or chambers: the senate and the house of representatives. The senate has fifty members, and the house of representatives has one hundred members. Senators are elected to a four-year term, and representatives to a two-year term. There is no limit on the number of terms a member of the legislature may serve.

Judicial

The Indiana Supreme Court is the highest court in the state. It has five judges, called justices. One of the five is the chief justice. The state also has a court of appeals with fifteen judges—three for each of the state's five districts. The supreme court and the court of appeals are appellate courts: they review whether or not the decisions made in the lower courts were fair and without error. Another appellate court is the tax court, which deals specifically with tax cases. Lower courts that conduct trials include the circuit courts and, in some counties, superior courts. There are also city and town courts in some counties. Appeals from city and town courts are heard in circuit and superior courts. In addition, Marion County has a small claims court, and St. Joseph County has a probate court, which deals with wills and related matters. Supreme court justices are picked by the governor, and after two years, citizens vote whether or not to keep the judge on the bench for another ten years.

Silly Law

According to Section 401-103 of the Indianapolis Municipal Code, it is illegal to collect rags, paper, or "general" junk before 7:30 a.m. or after 5:30 p.m. However, junking and rag picking are allowed within the boundaries of North Street, South Street, East Street, and West Street. But it is never allowed anywhere on Sunday.

How a Bill Becomes a Law

Indiana's legislators create laws and programs to help their districts and the state. In the legislative process, a law begins as a bill, which is a proposal, or suggestion, for a law. To reach its final form, a bill goes through a series of steps. If a bill is to become a law, it must pass every step.

David Long and Brian Bosma from the Indiana General Assembly address anti-discrimination safeguards in a religious freedom bill in 2015.

Any senator or representative may introduce a bill. There is one exception: bills for raising money must originate in the house of representatives. Often the idea for a bill comes from suggestions from voters. When bills are introduced, they proceed through one chamber at a time. The first step is to introduce a bill and read it to the chamber. If there is interest in pursuing the bill, it is sent to committee. The committee does research on the topic and holds hearings to listen to experts and voter opinions. After the hearing, the committee may vote on the bill or table it (take no action). If the committee tables the bill, it will die unless the committee votes on it later. If the committee approves the bill by a majority vote, the bill advances.

The bill is then read a second time to the chamber, and any member may propose changes or amendments to the bill. Amendments must be approved by a simple majority of votes. Once the changes are included in the bill, it is put to another vote. If it again passes, it is set to be read for a third time. In the third reading, changes can be made, but approval of the changes must come from a two-thirds majority. If the final changes are approved, then the entire bill is voted on and a simple majority is needed to win. Once approved in the original chamber, the bill is sent to the other chamber. If approved there with no changes, then the bill is sent to the governor to sign into law. If the second chamber makes changes, then the bill must be returned to the original chamber for approval. If there is conflict, the bill is sent to a conference committee made up of two legislators from each chamber. If a compromise is reached by the committee and agreed upon by the two chambers, the bill goes before the governor who can sign it, veto it, or take no action. If no action is taken for seven days, then the bill becomes law. If it is vetoed, legislators can override the veto if they can achieve majority approval of both chambers. Rarely does vetoed legislation become law. Once the bill has been enacted, it is assigned to the secretary of state, who gives the bill a number and enters it into the legislative code.

POLITICAL FIGURES
FROM INDIANA

⭐ Birch Bayh Jr.: US Senator, 1963-1981

Senator Birch Bayh Jr. wrote the Twenty-Fifth and Twenty-Sixth Amendments to the Constitution and the Title IX Higher Education Act, which prohibited discrimination against females in academic and sports programs. He is the only person not among the founding fathers to have written two constitutional amendments.

⭐ André Carson: US House of Representatives, 2008-

The Indianapolis native is the second Muslim to serve in the House of Representatives. He has been a member of several committees, including the House Select Permanent Committee on Intelligence. He sponsored bills to help members of the military financially and with their mental health. He is also a member of the Congressional Black Caucus's Executive Leadership Team.

⭐ J. Danforth Quayle: Vice President of the United States, 1989-1993

Before becoming vice president, Dan Quayle served two terms in the US House of Representatives and two in the US Senate. A native of Indianapolis, he served one term as vice president under President George H. W. Bush. He was chairman of the National Space Council and made forty-seven visits to foreign countries.

INDIANA
YOU CAN MAKE A DIFFERENCE

Contacting Lawmakers

To find contact information for the state and federal legislators who represent Indiana, go to the website: **iga.in.gov/legislative/find-legislators**. Fill in your address and click "Search." The names of your representatives in the state senate and house of representatives, the US Senate, and the US House of Representatives will pop up. Contact information appears alongside a photograph of the legislator. The website also provides information about bills and laws.

Rescuing Recess

Over the course of many years, public school budgets have grown tighter, and teachers and students have felt the stress of teaching and studying for standardized tests. What has been cut in many schools has been recess and physical activity. Parents and teachers in Indiana recognized that students were more alert, happier, and less fidgety if they were allowed recess during the school day, so they drafted a petition and delivered it to the Indiana state legislature. They teamed up with a national program co-sponsored by the Cartoon Network and the National PTA (Parent-Teacher Association), called "Rescuing Recess." Students sent letters to the state legislature and parents, teachers, and concerned citizens signed petitions, in part stating, "We the people, general citizens, educators, parents and concerned parties are asking the Indiana Legislature to mandate at least (2) recesses in Indiana Schools consisting of at least 15 minutes each, once before lunch and once after lunch."

The petition and the letter-writing campaign convinced state senators to propose a bill, SB 111, which required schools to "provide daily physical activity for students in elementary school." The first reading was on January 9, 2006. Then the bill was sent to committee. On January 12, 2006, SB 111 passed and became law. In 2010, additions to the law required health, nutrition, and physical education programs for all grades.

Toyota is one of many carmakers that help Indiana remain one of the country's leaders in automobile production.

Making a Living

Indiana has a reputation for being an agricultural state, and people working in agriculture make a significant contribution to the economy. Other activities contribute to the state economy as well, however. People work in manufacturing, service jobs, life sciences, transportation, and mining. In Indiana, the proportion of the workforce working in manufacturing is greater than in any other state.

Agriculture Today

Farms are found throughout Indiana. Even urban counties, such as Marion and Lake Counties, have farmland. Soil, rainfall, and hot summers make Indiana farmland very productive.

Of all the agricultural products, corn brings in the most income. Soybeans are second, and hogs are third. Much of those harvests are used as animal feed for Indiana's hogs and other livestock. Corn is also sold as fresh ears and popcorn. More than 20 percent of the nation's popcorn is grown in Indiana.

Indiana farmers grow tomatoes, cantaloupes, and watermelons, which thrive in the sandy soil of southwestern Indiana. Winter wheat, potatoes, hay, cucumbers, green beans, and onions are important crops. Apples, peaches, and blueberries are also grown.

Farmers earn additional income by allowing wind turbines to be placed in their fields.

Poultry farms raise chickens, ducks, and turkeys. Some poultry farms specialize in eggs and baby chick production. Ice cream is a leading dairy product. Indiana's meatpacking industry processes hogs, cattle, sheep, and poultry.

Manufacturing

Indiana's factories make and process a wide range of products. The Calumet region of northwest Indiana is known for the production of high-quality steel. To make the steel, ingredients such as iron, coke, and limestone are heated in blast furnaces. Coke is coal that has been baked until it is almost pure carbon. Steel beams, household and medical appliances, machinery, and motor vehicles and parts are some of the things made of steel.

Indiana is a leader in the production of auto parts. Its factories turn out brakes, axles, pistons, exhaust pipes, carburetors, and electrical components for cars and trucks. Manufacturing plants make diesel engines for buses and heavy-duty construction equipment. Some make bodies for delivery vans, trucks, ambulances, and shuttle buses. Other plants assemble cars and trucks. Recreational vehicles are a specialty of Indiana's automotive industry.

Many homes are built using Indiana lumber and other forest products.

Major pharmaceutical companies manufacture drugs and operate laboratories in Indiana. They do research on treatments for humans and animals. The pharmaceutical company Eli Lilly and Company is one of the largest employers in Indiana. The company has a history of medical breakthroughs, such as being the first company to sell insulin as a treatment for diabetes.

Indiana's hardwood forests supply wood used in house construction and to make furniture. Trees such as oak, maple, cherry, and walnut are cut into thin layers of veneer. Veneer is used to cover furniture to give it beauty. Pulp made from scraps and odd pieces of wood is turned into paper products. Each step of the manufacturing process adds value to the wood and creates jobs.

Unfortunately, in recent years, a number of Indiana factories have closed. In many cases, the factories were important employers in their communities, and factory shutdowns cause severe hardship for the people who once worked in those plants. When the Whirlpool Corporation closed its refrigerator factory in Evansville in 2010, more than one thousand people lost their jobs. However, Indiana does not depend on one industry to supply manufacturing jobs, so it remains a leader in manufacturing employment. It did not suffer like Michigan did when that state lost jobs in automobile manufacturing. In 2015, manufacturing generated 30 percent of the state's economic output, way above the national average of 12 percent.

Mining

Limestone may be the most widely known mineral that is mined in Indiana. The light gray or light tan stone covers many important buildings in the state and in the nation. Limestone is also carved into statues and into building elements such as columns and decorative molding. Limestone is cut from quarries located in south-central Indiana.

Another material mined in Indiana is coal. It is taken mostly from strip mines in the southwestern part of the state. Sand, gravel, clay, and shale are also widely collected. Limestone, sand, shale, and iron oxide are combined to make cement. Indiana also produces small amounts of oil and natural gas.

★ 10 KEY ★ INDUSTRIES

Hogs

Life Sciences

1. Automotive Manufacturing

Indiana is the second-largest state in cars and automotive parts manufacturing. Japanese carmakers Toyota, Subaru, and Honda, and General Motors and Chrysler have manufacturing plants in Indiana. In 2014, this industry generated $9.9 billion.

2. Chicken Eggs

Many small farms raise chickens for eggs, which they sell directly to consumers. Large farms supply grocery stores and restaurants. Small farmers average about 70,000 dozen eggs a year and large farms about 440 million dozen eggs a year.

3. Dairy Farming

There are more than 1,200 dairy farms in Indiana, and 97 percent are family owned, with average herd sizes of 129 cows. Dairy farming provides more than $810 million and 8,220 jobs for Indiana's economy. Ice cream production ranks second in the nation.

4. Hogs

The pork industry is the largest livestock industry in Indiana. Farmers receive $40 to $60 per head. Indiana is more successful than other hog-producing states because most of its hog farms are family owned and can make adjustments easier than corporate farms.

5. Life Sciences

Indiana's life sciences industry—pharmaceuticals, medical devices, biotechnology, and agricultural research—earns $59 billion annually. Indiana is the global headquarters for major firms, including Cook Medical, Biomet, and Eli Lilly.

6. Mining

There are nearly three hundred active mining operations in Indiana, providing jobs to sixteen thousand people. About $2 billion worth of raw materials, such as coal, aluminum, lime, and gypsum, have been mined annually in recent years.

7. Recreational Vehicles

Elkhart County is a leading producer of campers, trailers, and motor homes. It is home to well-known brands such as Coachman, Shasta, Jayco, Forest River, and Thor. In 2014, Indiana shipped 33,843 recreational vehicles.

8. Row Crops

Row crops, such as soybeans, corn, and wheat, produced an income of $1.7 billion in 2015. Although prices have recently dropped slightly, production has gone up due to new technology, such as drones with cameras that can inspect distant fields.

9. Services

Workers in service industries earn a combined $110 billion. Health care leads the industry, with workers earning $14 billion annually. Other occupations include retail, food service, wholesaling, and transportation, as well as banking, insurance, and professional workers, such as lawyers and architects.

10. Steel

Indiana is the nation's leading steel producer, combining with Chicago to make more than 34 million tons (30.8 million metric tons). More than 180,000 Indianans make raw steel or finished products, such as construction beams and automotive parts. Others work in research and development, sales, and shipping.

Recreational Vehicles

Row Crops

Recipe for Hoosier Corn Casserole

What You Need

Large skillet

11-by-7-inch (28-by-18 cm) casserole dish

Cheese grater

Kitchen knife

Measuring cups and spoons

Mixing bowl and spoon

Fork

1 medium green pepper, chopped

2 green onions, sliced

1 tablespoon (15 milliliters) butter

1 teaspoon (5 mL) cooking oil

3 tablespoon (45 mL) bacon bits

3 eggs

½ cup (118 mL) sour cream

½ cup (118 mL) whole milk

¼ cup (31 grams) all-purpose flour

½ teaspoon (2.5 mL) salt

¼ teaspoon (1.25 mL) pepper

4 cups (0.9 liters) frozen corn, thawed

1 cup (114 g) shredded cheddar cheese

2 medium tomatoes

What To Do

- Heat oven to 350°F (177°C).
- Grate cheese and set aside.
- With the help of an adult, chop green onions. Set aside.
- Slice green peppers. Set aside.
- Chop tomatoes. Set aside.
- In skillet, add oil and butter and cook green pepper and onion over medium heat until tender. Add bacon bits, cook 1 minute more. Set aside.
- In bowl, beat eggs with fork. Stir in sour cream, milk, flour, salt, and pepper.
- Stir in corn, onions, peppers, and half of the cheese.
- Bake for 25 minutes.
- Sprinkle tomatoes and the remaining cheese on top.
- Bake 5 minutes more.
- Carefully remove from oven and let cool a few minutes before serving.

Transportation

Highways, railroads, airports, and ports for ships all help Indiana's farmers and manufacturers to reach their customers. These passageways connect Indiana's cities and towns with Chicago, Illinois, and Louisville, Kentucky, as well as with more distant transportation hubs throughout the nation. Trucks travel the interstate highways that run east-west across northern, central, and southern Indiana and north-south through Indianapolis. Railroads converge on Indianapolis, too. Indiana has three major ports. Two are on the Ohio River, at Mount Vernon and Jeffersonville. One is on Lake Michigan, at Burns Harbor in Portage. These ports handle large shipments of grain, coal, steel, and fertilizer. Many ships leaving these ports travel all the way to the Atlantic Ocean or the Gulf of Mexico. The Lake Michigan port handles the most oceangoing cargo of any US port on the Great Lakes.

Highways help people get to and from work and relaxing recreation areas. They also attract businesses and jobs to the areas they pass through. A number of

In Their Own Words

"The quality of life here is much better than many other urban communities, and there have been plenty of employment opportunities. Many come here for that reason, particularly families."
—Monica Medina, board president of La Plaza, an Indianapolis non-profit

New highways will help products from rural areas of Indiana get to consumers quickly.

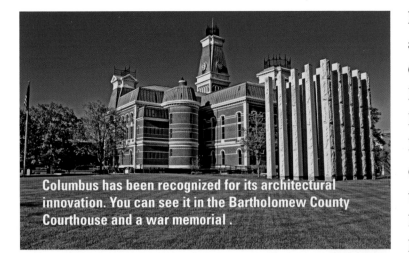
Columbus has been recognized for its architectural innovation. You can see it in the Bartholomew County Courthouse and a war memorial .

high-technology companies are situated along Interstate 65, near West Lafayette and Purdue University, and along Interstate 69 in northeastern Indiana. Interstate 69 is being extended from Indianapolis to Evansville in the southwest. Near Evansville, the new highway will use an existing road, Interstate 164, which extends about 21 miles (34 km) north of town. A section from Crane to Bloomington opened in December 2015. People hope the new highway will draw businesses and new residents to southern Indiana and give the state economy a boost.

Service Jobs

Service jobs involve practicing a special skill or helping another individual or business. Service workers, for example, provide medical or dental care, business management, and legal advice. They perform jobs such as sales, computer programming, and accounting. They make car repairs and do cleaning. In Indiana, health-care workers, businesspeople, office workers, and food-service workers are among the most numerous types of service workers.

Other service workers include the state's many counselors, teachers, and scientists. Scientists usually have jobs in government agencies, companies, or colleges or universities. Teachers generally work in private or public schools or in colleges or universities.

Tourism

Tourism is another key service industry. The people who work in hotels, restaurants, and stores that tourists visit are service workers. So are workers such as museum staff members and tour guides. Indiana has many tourist attractions. Some are part of the National Park Service—such as the Indiana Dunes National Lakeshore on Lake Michigan, the George Rogers Clark National Historical Park at Vincennes, and the Lincoln Boyhood National Memorial at Lincoln City. The Hoosier National Forest in south-central Indiana has interesting caves and karst features. There also are three national wildlife refuges and dozens of state parks and forests located throughout Indiana.

Indianapolis's children's museum is the biggest in the world. The city is also home to other major museums, including the Indianapolis Museum of Art, the Eiteljorg Museum of

American Indians and Western Art, the Indiana State Museum, and the Benjamin Harrison Presidential Site.

Indiana's many history-related attractions include the Conner Prairie Interactive History Park. Located in Fishers, near Indianapolis, it offers an outdoor re-creation of nineteenth-century life. The Indianapolis Symphony Orchestra plays at the park in the summer. Aviation pioneer Wilbur Wright was born in Indiana in 1867. His restored birthplace home, which is near Hagerstown, is now a museum.

Because of the state's long association with the automobile industry, there are many museums that attract car and racing buffs, such as the Auburn Cord Duesenberg Automobile Museum in Auburn, the Studebaker National Museum in South Bend, and the Hall of Fame Museum at the Indianapolis Motor Speedway.

The speedway itself is one of the state's greatest attractions. Car racing, however, is only one of the favorite sports pastimes of both Indianans and visitors to the state. Football and especially basketball are popular. The state's professional teams include the Pacers in the National Basketball Association, the Fever in the Women's National Basketball Association, and the Colts in the National Football League. All three are based in Indianapolis. People are passionate about Indiana University basketball. Fans of sports history flock to museums such as the Indiana Basketball Hall of Fame at New Castle and the College Football Hall of Fame in South Bend. High school basketball is very popular, with more than twenty thousand people attending the boys' finals each year.

Working Together

The people of Indiana have used the resources of their state to make it a leader in agriculture and in manufacturing. They continue to invent products that are used throughout the nation and the world. People in transportation are working to develop the best ways for Indiana to send its products to faraway places. More and more, scientists and businesspeople in Indiana work together. They combine their ideas and knowledge to develop new ways to create products that will improve health care and agriculture. The energy and creativity of the people of Indiana have helped to make the state a good place to work and to live.

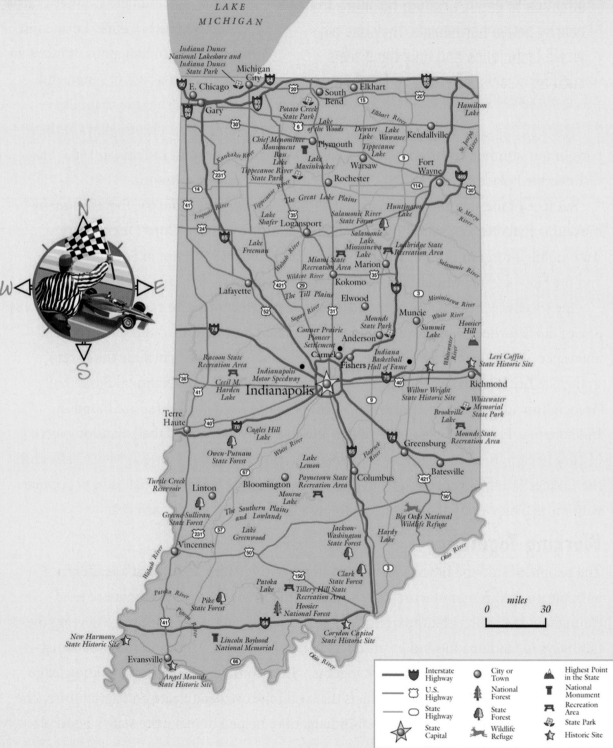

LAKE MICHIGAN

Indiana Dunes National Lakeshore and Indiana Dunes State Park

Michigan City

E. Chicago

Gary

South Bend

Elkhart

Hamilton Lake

Potato Creek State Park

Lake of the Woods

Elkhart River

Dewart Lake

Kendallville

Chief Menominee Monument

Bass Lake

Plymouth

Lake Wawasee

St. Joseph River

Tippecanoe River State Park

Lake Maxinkuckee

Tippecanoe Lake

Warsaw

Fort Wayne

Kankakee River

Rochester

The Great Lake Plains

Huntington Lake

Iroquois River

Lake Shafer

Logansport

Salamonie River State Forest

St. Marys River

Salamonie Lake

Lake Freeman

Wabash River

Mississinewa Lake

Lothridge State Recreation Area

Salamonie River

Miami State Recreation Area

Marion

Wildcat River

Lafayette

The Till Plains

Kokomo

Missinewa River

Squaw River

Elwood

Muncie

White River

Hoosier Hill

Mounds State Park

Summit Lake

Conner Prairie Pioneer Settlement

Anderson

Indiana Basketball Hall of Fame

Levi Coffin State Historic Site

Racoon State Recreation Area

Carmel

Fishers

Cecil M. Harden Lake

Indianapolis Motor Speedway

Indianapolis

Wilbur Wright State Historic Site

Richmond

Whitewater Memorial State Park

Brookville Lake

Terre Haute

Cagles Mill Lake

White River

Mounds State Recreation Area

Owen-Putnam State Forest

Lake Lemon

Greensburg

Batesville

Turtle Creek Reservoir

Linton

Bloomington

Paynetown State Recreation Area

Columbus

Monroe Lake

Flatrock River

Greene-Sullivan State Forest

Big Oaks National Wildlife Refuge

Lake Greenwood

Jackson-Washington State Forest

Hardy Lake

Vincennes

Clark State Forest

Ohio River

Patoka Lake

Pike State Forest

Tillery Hill State Recreation Area

Patoka River

Hoosier National Forest

Petoka River

Corydon Capitol State Historic Site

New Harmony State Historic Site

Lincoln Boyhood National Memorial

Evansville

Ohio River

Angel Mounds State Historic Site

miles
0   30

Interstate Highway		City or Town		Highest Point in the State
U.S. Highway		National Forest		National Monument
State Highway		State Forest		Recreation Area
State Capital		Wildlife Refuge		State Park
				Historic Site

INDIANA

MAP SKILLS

1. How many interstate highways enter Indianapolis?

2. What two interstate highways would you take to travel between the first capital of Indiana and the present capital?

3. What city is closest to East Chicago?

4. The city of Vincennes lies along what river?

5. Which city is closer to Indianapolis: Columbus or Fort Wayne?

6. Is Linton east or west of Bloomington?

7. Which river runs through Indianapolis?

8. Which is farther north: Angel Mounds State Historic Site or Tippecanoe River State Park?

9. Is South Bend north or south of Kokomo?

10. What city is closest to the confluence of the Saint Joseph and the Saint Marys Rivers?

Interstate 65

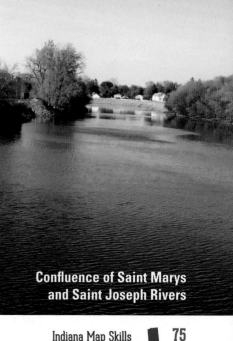

Confluence of Saint Marys and Saint Joseph Rivers

1. Four
2. I-64 and I-65
3. Gary
4. Wabash River
5. Columbus
6. West
7. White River
8. Tippecanoe River State Park
9. North
10. Fort Wayne

State Flag, Seal, and Song

At the center of the Indiana state flag is a torch standing for liberty and enlightenment, which is surrounded by thirteen stars, representing the original thirteen states. The half-circle of five stars represent the next five states to join the Union. The large star above the torch represents Indiana.

The state seal is circular. An outer band reads "Seal of the State of Indiana" and the date 1816. On each side of the date is a diamond and two tulip tree leaves. In the inner circle are two sycamore trees and a man raising an ax. On the left, a buffalo jumps over a log into green grass. In the background, the sun shines above three hills.

"On the Banks of the Wabash, Far Away" is the Indiana state song. It was written by Paul Dresser of Terre Haute, who published it in July 1897. The Indiana General Assembly adopted the song as the official state song on March 14, 1913. It is the oldest state symbol, having been adopted four years before the state flag.

To view the lyrics of the Indiana state song, visit: **secure.in.gov/history/2800.htm**

Glossary

confluence   The junction of two rivers, especially rivers of approximately equal width.

conservation   The careful use of natural resources to prevent them from being lost or wasted.

deciduous   A type of tree that sheds its leaves seasonally.

endangered   Describing something that is at risk of dying off.

extinct   Describing a plant or animal species that is no longer in existence.

flyway   A route regularly used by large numbers of migrating birds.

fossil   A preserved remnant of a plant or animal from an older geologic age.

glaciers   Slowly moving masses of ice and rock.

invasive species   A non-native species that spreads rapidly and takes over the habitat of a native species.

karst   Landscape caused by the erosion of limestone. This creates ridges, towers, sinkholes, and other formations.

missionaries   People who go to another place to spread religious beliefs and/or to help people who are poor or sick.

moraine   A mass of rocks and sediment deposited by a glacier.

nomads   People who move from place to place, taking their belongings with them.

portage   A trail used by people to carry their boats between two bodies of water.

watershed   The area of land that includes a particular river or lake and all the rivers, streams, and springs that flow into it.

More About Indiana

BOOKS

Katz, William Loren. *Black Pioneers: An Untold Story*. New York: Atheneum Books for Young People, 1999.

Stille, Darlene R. *Indiana*. America the Beautiful. New York: Children's Press, 2014.

Wyckoff, Edwin Brit. *The Man Who Invented Television: The Genius of Philo T. Farnsworth*. Berkeley Heights, NJ: Enslow Elementary, 2013.

WEBSITES

Indiana Department of Nature Resources

secure.in.gov/dnr/naturepreserve/

Indiana Dunes National Lakeshore

www.nps.gov/indu

Indiana Historical Society Online Tour

www.destination-indiana.com/

The Official Indiana State Website

www.in.gov

ABOUT THE AUTHORS

Kathleen Derzipilski is a research editor who specializes in nonfiction. She lives in San Diego, California.

Richard Hantula is a writer and editor who lives in New York City. He was the senior US editor for the *Macmillan Encyclopedia of Science*.

Ruth Bjorklund lives on Bainbridge Island, near Seattle, Washington, with her family. She has written numerous books for young people and is thankful to have visited every state.

Index

Page numbers in **boldface** are illustrations. Entries in **boldface** are glossary terms.

African Americans, 33, 36, 39–40, 47, **47**, 50–51
American Revolution, **22**, 25–26, 43
Amish, **44**, 53, 73
Archaic tradition, 23

Battle of Tippecanoe, 28–29
Bloomington, 13, 35, 46, 48, 51–52, 66, 72

Calumet region, 16, 38–39, 50–51, 66
canals, 14, 32–34, 46
Civil War, 36–37, 39
climate, 17–18
Coffin, Levi and Catharine, 33, **33**
confluence, 34
conservation, 18

deciduous, 9, **9**
dunes, **6**, 8–9, 14, 16, 35, 39, 72

education, 51–53, 59, 63, 72
Eiteljorg Museum, 42, 54, 72–73
endangered, 19
Evansville, 14, 32, 34, 39–40, 46, 67, 72
extinct, 19

farming, **8**, 12, 15, 18, 26–27, 31, 37–38, 40, 46, 55, 65–66, **66**, 68–69, 71, 73
flyway, 18
forests, 4, 9, 12, 14–15, 20–21, 27, 37, 67, 72
Fort Wayne, 13, 32, 34, 41, 46, 48, 66
fossil, 5, **17**
French and Indian War, 25–26

Gary, 35, 39, 40–41, 46, 48, 50
glaciers, 7–8, 16
glassmaking, 35, 38
government
    federal, 25, 27–28, 32, 40–41, 45, 58, 62
    local, **56**, 57–58, 60
    state, 5, 28–29, 32, 52, 57–61, 63
Grange, the, 37–38

Harrison, William Henry, 28–29, **28**
Hispanics, 50–51

Indianapolis, 12, 14, 32, 34–35, 41–43, **42**, 46, 48–49, 54–55, 58, **58**, 60, 62, 71–73
Indianapolis Motor Speedway, 38, 43, 55, 73
Indiana University, 35, 42, 52, 73
invasive species, 12, 19

Karner blue butterfly, 19, **19**
karst, 8, 72
Ku Klux Klan, 39–40, **39**

Lake Michigan, **6**, 7–9, 14, 16, 24, 35, 39, 71–72
La Salle, René-Robert Cavelier, sieur de, 24, **25**
limestone, 5, 8, 55, 66–67

Index

Lincoln, Abraham, 31, **31**, 36, 72

manufacturing, **36**, 37–38, 40, 46–47, 50, 55, **64**, 65–69, 71, 73
Miami (tribe), 5, 14, 24, 26–28, **27**, 32, 43, 51
mining, 35, 46–47, 55, 65, 67, 69
missionaries, 24
Mississippian tradition, 23
moraine, 16
mounds, 14, 23, 43
Mount Baldy, **6**, 9, 14
Muncie, 35, 38, 46, **56**

Native Americans, 5, 14, 16, 24–29, **24**, **28**, 32, 43, 45, 50–52, 54
natural gas, 38, 67
nomads, 14, 43
Northwest Territory, 25, 28, 43, 45, 50

portage, 14, 16
Potawatomi, 15, 24, 26, 32
prairie, 9, 12, 14, 19–20

Purdue University, 12, 49, 52, 72

railroads, 32–34, 37, 39, 46, 51, 71
rivers
    Illinois, 13, 16
    Maumee, 13, 24, 34
    Ohio, 7, 12–14, 16, **16**, **17**, **22**, 23, 25, 31, 40, 71
    Saint Joseph, 13, 16, 24, 34
    Saint Marys, 13, 24, 34
    Tippecanoe, 15, 16, 28
    Wabash, 5, 12–13, 16, 23–25, 28

settlers, 5, 14–15, 24–25, 28–29, 31, 34–35, 43, 45, 52–53
slavery, 31, 33, 36–37, 43, 50
South Bend, 6–17, 34, 36, 46, 53, 73
sports, 34, 42–43, **46**, 49, 53–54, 73
steel, 35, **37**, 38–40, 47, 51, 66, 69, 71

Tecumseh, 28–29, **28**
tornadoes, 18, 41–42, **41**
tourism, 14–15, **29**, 34, 54, 72–73

Underground Railroad, 33
Unigov, 58
University of Notre Dame, 34, 52–53

Vincennes, **22**, 25, 28, 43, 52, 72

watershed, 13
WASPs, 41
Woodland tradition, 23
World War II, 40–41, 49